BERNAND WARLEY

PLOT GARDENING

The Ultimate Guide on How to Create the Most Beautiful Garden, Learn Tips and Tricks on How You Can Have A Garden You Can Be Really Proud Of!

Descrierea CIP a Bibliotecii Naţionale a României
BERNAND WARLEY
    PLOT GARDENING. The Ultimate Guide on How to Create the Most Beautiful Garden, Learn Tips and Tricks on How You Can Have A Garden You Can Be Really Proud Of! / Bernand Warley. – Bucharest: Editura My Ebook, 2020
    ISBN

BERNAND WARLEY

PLOT GARDENING

The Ultimate Guide on How to Create the Most Beautiful Garden, Learn Tips and Tricks on How You Can Have A Garden You Can Be Really Proud Of!

My Ebook Publishing House
Bucharest, 2020

CONTENTS

Gardening Tips: Borders 7

General Gardening Tips 9

Late Autumn Gardening Tips 11

Gardening Tips: Using The Internet 13

Gardening Tips: More Advice 15

What Kind Of Landscaping Equipment Do You Need
To Have Around The House? 17

Find Yourself A Great Landscaping Picture 20

Why Use Landscaping Stones? 23

Get The Best Around The Pool Landscaping 26

Rain And Snow In Your Yard Landscaping 28

A Wonderful Backyard Landscaping Idea 31

Free Landscaping Software Helps Design Exterior On A
Budget 34

Hillside Landscaping: Make That Hill Look Beautiful!... 37

Landscaping Pictures Offer Different Possibilities 40

Low Maintenance Landscaping Chicago 43

The Key To Landscaping Design 45

What Does Your Landscaping Plan Need? 47

Not All Landscaping Software Is Created Equal 49

Do You Know How To Choose The Right Landscaping Supply Store? 52

Pool Landscaping Will Require Significant Thought 54

Gardening Tips: Growing Hot Peppers 57

Gardening Tips: Starting A Butterfly Garden 60

Gardening Tips: Compost 63

Gardening Tips: Organic Gardening 66

Gardening Tips: Patio Gardening 69

Gardening Tips: Winter Gardening 72

Gardening Tips: Creating A Wildlife Garden 75

Gardening Tips: Common Pests 78

Gardening Tips: Types Of Soil 81

Gardening Tips: Starting With A New Garden 84

Florist – Use Them For The Floral/Flower Gardening Idea 87

Indoor Gardening Supplies For Winter Fun 91

Cast Iron Furniture 94

Gardening Catalog 98

Gardening 101

Raised Summer Gardens 104

Landscaping Your Summer Garden 108

Oak Garden Furniture 112

Picking A Healthy Plant 115

Picking The Ideal Location For Your Garden 119

Summer Garden Weddings 122

Understanding Container Gardening 125

GARDENING TIPS: BORDERS

If you want to add ground cover such as creeping thyme or alyssum to your garden here is a great way to get started early and a fabulous way to create instant borders without the backache of having to plant each flower. Measure the area you want covered with ground cover. Let's say you want to create a border along an existing garden that is 10 feet long. Cut newspaper (about 2 pages thick) into two feet long by one foot wide strips. To cover 10 feet you will need five of these two foot strips. Place the strips in a slightly sunny area but where the seeds won't be disturbed or pelted with rays of light, such as basement shelving near a window. Place garbage bags on the shelves then add the newspaper strips. Do not overlap strips.

Sprinkle the seeds on the newspaper like you would if you were planting them in the ground. Place a layer of paper towel over each strip and then spray the towel, seeds and newspaper with a water bottle. You want to saturate the towel and the newspaper, but you don't want it to drip. The paper must never dry out (if it does spray immediately.) Remove the paper towel when the seeds germinate (in about a week.) Two months later, weather permitting, you can plant your newspaper strips, now bursting with seedlings, outdoors. First carefully arrange each seedling strip where it will be planted. Once you are happy with the arrangement cover bare newspaper areas with soil to anchor the strip.

GENERAL GARDENING TIPS

Save all flats and flower pots that come with your plants. First, you can always use these to start your seeds next season (be sure to wash the flats to rid them of any disease.) Second, it may look funny at first, but if you cut out the bottom of plastic pots and place them over younger transplants it will protect them from rabbits. Additionally, placing pots around ornamental grasses is a great way to contain the younger, lower grass strands from rotting as they lay on the ground. The band created by the pot will keep the strands off the ground.

Here's a coffee tip. Humans are not the only ones to get a boost from espresso. Plants do too! Caffeine and theophylline, two ingredients of coffee are popular ingredients in expensive skin care products, and key ingredients in asthma medications, but also make excellent fertilizer for plants. You can get it by the big bagful and for free just by contacting your local coffee shop.

Just mix the espresso in with your existing soil every few months and watch your plants grow. Successful gardening means that you don't always have to buy everything new, such as pots or fertilizer. Look around your home to see what you already have that you can reuse.

LATE AUTUMN GARDENING TIPS

Come fall gardeners are usually a little teary-eyed over parting ways with garden tasks. For a little late season planting run to the nearest garden section and buy California poppy, candytuft, cornflower, dianthus, phlox, cosmos, soapwort, spinach, larkspur, pansies, some marigolds, snapdragons, garlic, and/or sweet pea seeds for what should be half off at that time of year.

These hardy annuals can actually be planted in the fall and will bloom in the spring or summer!

Who doesn't want instant blooming results in the garden? If you buy a plant you want it to be all it can be like, yesterday, right. Nurseries know this and so you will pay a premium for larger plants. Not only is there a demand, but also the overhead on a mature plant is more than a new one (larger container, more water, etc.) But if you are patient, buy the smaller plant. It will save you a good deal of money and in a couple of months, with the right conditions and some Miracle grow your plant formerly known as small, will be a force to be reckoned with.

Autumn is a great time of year to buy your seeds on sale as well as plant those late year garden varieties in your garden. Take the time to plan an autumn garden so you can enjoy flowers late into the year.

GARDENING TIPS: USING THE INTERNET

The Internet is a gardener's best friend. You might be surprised to know that your local nursery has been charging you way too much money. Or you might be pleasantly surprised to discover your local nursery is the best kept secret with great prices and stock. The point is, shop around online as well as offline. Here is one reason why: while searching for farmers or companies that sold plants in her area, one gardener we interviewed came across a nursery she had never heard of. She called and discovered they sold directly to nurseries until June when they opened to the public, but since she was local she could look through their 12 greenhouses and buy what she wanted. She had her pick of flowers, colors, textures, and rarities and didn't have to worry about the item she wanted being sold out. Not only can you find great deals by researching, but you can also find new sources!

As well, the Internet is a great place to get ideas for next year's garden. You'll find many ideas no matter what type of garden you're growing. Check out gardening forums to see what other gardeners around the country are doing. You might find a great new garden idea that is sure to transform your garden into a neighborhood show piece.

GARDENING TIPS: MORE ADVICE

Stones between the sizes of oranges and cantaloupes make great decorations, or borders for gardens, but if you want a lot they can be costly. If you live near new construction, be it a large building or a new neighborhood, you are sure to find many suitable rocks for your garden. Be careful, as construction sites can be dangerous. Don't forget to bring a wagon with so you can easily roam the area and move your stones at the same time.

Here's a tip about plants and seeds. Whether the plant is an annual, perennial, or bush such as the azalea you should harvest the seeds even if you don't plan on planting them. Why?

Because you can trade them for other seeds, grow the plants and sell them at the end of your driveway or at the farmer's market for extra money. You can even donate the seeds to local charities, or animal shelters that can then resell them at a fundraiser.

Gardening is all about finding out what works best for you and what doesn't. Take the time to write down all of your gardening ideas so that you can read them over during the winter months in preparation for the spring months. Than when spring arrives you'll be ready to buy the seeds and plants you want for your new garden plan.

WHAT KIND OF LANDSCAPING EQUIPMENT DO YOU NEED TO HAVE AROUND THE HOUSE?

Is everything required?

Every little home would have a zest for that perfect landscaping. Not always do people hire professionals to have their landscaping done. At times you would have to just touch up the places where the water drifts or may be add minor layers. Even for trivial things as such, you would require to have the right equipments to proceed with your landscaping. There are certain fundamental equipments which you can't do without. Similarly, some others are not indispensible. There are also a few of the equipments which are filthy expensive and mostly is in possession of a professional landscaper. These are the ones worth being rented rather than spending hundreds and keeping it at the peace of your house for ceremonial activities of landscaping which may happen just few times in the year.

You have it, but did you know?

Fertilizer spreaders or other applicators essentially come under the category of landscaping equipments which perhaps you have, like most people do, but you are unaware of its logical landscaping use! People don't give it a thought about classifying them to be landscaping equipments. However, that is what these equipments effectively are! If you think you have such applicators but you don't apply them, then it is high time you start making use of them. Using them would make your yard look crimson and appealing with a healthier look. The turf would flourish and look lush not suffering from those upsetting weeds which outbreak innocently.

Getting towards stiff landscaping?

If you plan to do a lot of landscaping work yourself on your yard, then you would need quite a bit of those irrigational tools. This could either mean you are towards planting new foliage or any cultivation for that matter. Most of the shrubbery and flimsy flowers anticipate appropriate amount of water majority of the times. To get all this right, it is recommended that you invest on equipments like sprinklers and timers. They would ensure watering your yard even when you are not home. These things come handy especially when you have limited water resource for every other week.

Go about the right ones...

It is apparent that you wish that lush greenery within the scope of your yard. Landscaping equipments would assist with every exquisite idea of yours. To know what equipment is required for your landscaping activity, you can rely on the internet to advise you upon the same. Get the right equipments for your landscaping and experience the variation of ease.

FIND YOURSELF A GREAT LANDSCAPING PICTURE

Why landscaping picture?

Most often we would have a picture in our mind telling us how exquisite and different we want our landscaping to be done when compared to our neighbors. However, it would not be as easy to explain it to another person; why not a professional landscaper himself? When you go through various landscaping pictures, you get that clear-cut defining ability and you can elaborate as to what exactly you are looking for. Even if you have no notion about how the landscaping needs to be done, these pictures would give great inspirations to proceed further. Seldom do people have practical and suitable idea of landscaping when they are doing it new. So when you are choosing to renovate your landscaping activity next, ensure that you look for various pictures suiting what you have in mind.

Professional landscaper and landscaping pictures

Always ascertain that, however specialized is the landscaper you have chosen, at the very outset, he would show you different landscaping pictures. This would help you in knowing how the landscaper has an idea for the look of your house once the activity is completed. Such pictures would assist you in choosing the apt landscaper for having your job done as the picture they manifest would give you more information about them, such as their imagination and what work they plan to do. Consequently, always make the choice for your landscaper only after you have seen some interesting landscaping pictures.

Flip through the pictures

You should never forget to ask your landscaper about the different pictures of landscaping which he has done in the past. These are usually completed projects and they would give you an idea about your landscaper's proficiency at work. Experienced and the best of landscapers usually have more than one picture of their completed projects. They would also imply that you flip through their pictures portfolio and leave your decided choice up to them. Would this not give you abundant options to choose the right professional group?

Make the right choice

Landscaping would bestow upon that fabulous look of your house. Therefore, you would definitely want people passing by, to mention those affirmative statements as they observe your certified landscaping. A charming garden would give you not just what you are expecting, but more! Hence choose the right landscaper for your job deciding upon his pictures and lead the sport of perfect landscaping.

WHY USE LANDSCAPING STONES?

Why do you need them?

Several reasons fit in explaining why the landscaping stones are required in the overall design. The most apparent reason of course, is the esthetic beauty which would add to every other thing. Another reason for these landscaping stones is to maintain those neat layers which are hard to achieve without them.

Landscaping Stones work for amateur Landscaping

These stones give the required depth for your yard, and without much difficulty. Leveling up and down could be done even without the professional landscaping stones, i.e., by manual digging- landscaping. However, for this to be done, it would require you to know a lot about professional landscaping. Furthermore, it could lead to ruining your drainage system if you get into making blunders. Hence, it is always simpler to use these stones for getting depth within your yard.

The beauty factor

You can tone and touch up the yard with these stones around considerable portions. This can also involve planting foliage within them. Landscape stones look great around the lawn furniture and the fenced area. They also add the multihued colors in your yard as these stones come in different colors. During winters you would know the difference as the yard would otherwise be very bare looking and these stones would bejewel the area. Landscaping stones would no doubt give that total transformed look within your yard.

Sizes, Shapes and kinds

Landscaping stones come in all shapes and kinds as there is no dearth in the variety available. These stones when chosen in different sizes and colors give a variety affect within your yard. What is right and suits your yard would depend on the structure and plan of the yard. Most often, different parts of your yard would require different sizes of stones. Colors too, may vary and you can choose to mix different colors to give an exquisite and interesting look. These stones would help you to be creative so that your imagination could blend into their beauty for that new appeal in your yard.

If your yard is planned to get that refurbished look in the near future, then you may need to start searching for the colors and designs for the perfect landscaping. This would get the entire yard coordinated bringing tranquility and balance within the garden.

Landscaping stones could be found at any typical gardening joints or sometimes even the home building stores too. If you put an effort to shop around a bit, you would get those perfect landscaping stones to suit your yard and mind.

GET THE BEST AROUND
THE POOL LANDSCAPING

Utilizing around the pool landscaping would no doubt give a stunning look to your pool. This would not just transform an uninteresting piece of patch to be a starry one, but also bring a zest of Hollywood in your backyard.

Give an essence of brick, foliage, and stones: A fine pool landscaping blueprint would undeniably get your pool in the midst of appeal and create a magnetic lure in your yard. Striking brick walkways towards the yard, around the pool, could be considered in case of bigger yards. This notion could be led to other fractions of the yard too. Patio furniture along with tables and chairs can be placed on larger assemblage of bricks, for that amazing look!

A touch of green patches could also be regarded in pool landscaping. Foliage would add the required oxygen and take away the limestone gaze from the picture. Brick always gives a softer looking touch in the image. It would always ensure a warm inviting look in your yard never getting the standoffish stare within. Furthermore, the greens would double the splendor of the brick as a pool landscaping tool.

It is also suggested that you toss a few landscaping stones about the plants and on the limits of the veranda so that they get the exquisiteness to the overall landscaping design. Petite and spiky stones would give another coat of marvel to your landscape signifying the magnificence.

Flowers: In addition, multihued flowers too, give that amazing look miraculously. Night blooming flora would be appropriate if you tend to spend lots of time besides the pool especially during the nights. This would make sure to surround you with splendid blooms and ample cologne no matter what time of the day it is! It is not just the sunlight that should be pampered! Collectively, these ideas would without a qualm make your pool landscaping paramount.

It is for all time implied to initiate such pool landscaping at the earliest. Despite the fact that most of it could be done independently, a few facets would demand professional help. Without a question, your acquaintances would be astounded when they become aware about your pool landscaping. So why not begin to implement it right away?

RAIN AND SNOW IN YOUR YARD LANDSCAPING

How do you begin?

In the landscaping activity, Rains and Snow would have a major participation. You need to take care of those myopic granules when you landscape your yard. At the outset, it is recommended that you refer various books and writings on the subject. This is essential so that you don't miss out facts and certain important cautions due to which it is possible that you may even end up ruining your yard!

Do you require a professional?

Landscaping of the yard has to be done with utmost interest paying due attention to rains and snow, plus not forgetting the drainage of course! In winters the yard tends to get too muddy with puddles all around when its maintenance is not appropriate. In such conditions, if they occur at all, then a professional help is generally implied. People can handle most of the Landscaping themselves; however, the yard would be up-to-date and look certified only when certain things are dealt by professionals.

Rains work diplomatically!

When you skillfully work on your landscaping of yard, you need to ensure that you are doing it in a way that when it pours, your plants are watered. Water can be fed to the entire foliage of your yard if the landscaping is flawless. This kind of mechanism could be implemented considering the levels of downpour at different times of the year so that the balance is maintained. The impact of this works especially during summers when the rains are less than enough!

The Pleasance of snow

Snow is another thing adding significance to your yard. Snow is as imperative as the rain is when professional landscaping is considered. Besides watering the greens, it also helps in keeping the soil warm in spite of its cooling effect. This conversely says every little plant lying under the snow stays healthy and breathing. Furthermore, the bulbs in the spring would pop up in wonderful appearance and color adding to the beauty of your yard and its landscaping.

The concluding tip

When it rains, just make sure that the water is leveled all over the yard. This is vital to the overall landscaping planned to be done. All that you are required to do is just stroll about the yard as it begins to pour. Observe how the rain puddles with other spots where it drains, so that you have your next job of landscaping at ease. This is not being tactful, but also the finest way to start. It would also let you know the kind of drainage required for your yard so that you can landscape accordingly.

It is apparent that at the end of the day it is only the pleasance of your yard that relieves you of the entire day's anxiety. So ascertain to landscape well and give an expert makeover with things right!

A WONDERFUL BACKYARD LANDSCAPING IDEA

There are many different backyard landscaping ideas. Some of the best backyard landscaping ideas arc the ones that can fit into just about any backyard landscaping project. You can spend days reading various backyard landscaping ideas and not find one that is just right for you and your backyard. But some ideas and components are classics, and will fit into most any backyard landscaping idea. It's all about how you use them! Some of the more perennial concepts are covered below.

Evergreens - Looking Good Year Round

Evergreens are always a safe choice for your backyard landscaping idea. The trees and shrubs of this type stay a beautiful green all year. While the gorgeous deciduous trees like maples and oaks are pretty in the spring and summer, and stunning in the fall, in the winter they can leave your backyard landscape looking barren and lifeless without some evergreens to liven things up.

Hardscape - The Framework of Your Landscape

In addition to trees and plants, you should never leave hardscape out of your backyard landscaping idea. Hardscape is things like fences, rocks, landscaping stones, and fountains. Most anything that is used in your backyard landscaping idea that doesn't grow is hardscape. The trick is to use this hardscape harmoniously with the trees and plants of your backyard landscaping idea. You could have pillars of rock, for instance, framing a maple tree in your backyard. This looks especially good when combined with an evergreen climbing vine on the pillars, keeping life in the backyard landscape even in the winter months. Use your imagination, and try to picture how your backyard landscaping idea will look at various times of the year.

Year Round is Key

When designing any backyard landscaping idea, the thing to keep foremost in your mind is that it must look good all year long. Clever use of evergreens and hardscape in addition to the more conventional flowers and deciduous trees can make your backyard landscape gorgeous year round.

Walls and Fences to Frame it all

Don't forget to use walls and fences in your backyard landscaping idea. Properly used, walls and fences can mean the difference between a cozy backyard landscape nook and a wide open, barren backyard landscape. Don't neglect those climbing vines here either! Screening with vines, or allowing just a hint of wall to show from underneath a mat of vines, can make a HUGE difference in the overall look of your backyard landscaping idea.

FREE LANDSCAPING SOFTWARE HELPS DESIGN EXTERIOR ON A BUDGET

When working on a landscape design on a budget, you probably will not want to spend hundreds of dollars on 3D landscaping software. Some landscape companies offer free software that can be used to visualize the way different plants and colors would look to get the most out of your yard's available space. Most packages include many different types of plants, both annual and perennial, and allow the designer to alter the sizes of the plants for a more accurate picture of the finished design.

One of the main drawbacks to going with free landscaping software is that you may not be able to changes the house, the layout of the yard, or other things along those lines. In many packages, there is one house and a landscaping layout that cannot be changed. if this doesn't happen to match your house and yard, the software is only useful for choosing colors of flowers and type of plants.

This type of free landscaping software is usually offered by various companies selling flowers, seeds, and other landscaping products. Often the packages are designed specifically to showcase a company's particular products or breeds of plants. But with the cost of a very basic landscaping software package at over $100, living with the limitations can be worth it for the designer on a budget. There is no reason you can't use the software to choose your plants and things, then go purchase them at a local nursery or landscape supply store.

The lack of user-configurable options can be very obvious in these free landscaping software packages. Where complete landscaping software packages will include options and settings for adding in landscaping stones or lumber, the free versions usually do not include this ability. The company that provides the software determines what options are available to users of the software. You can try and see if a particular do-it-yourself landscape company offers some better free landscaping software that will allow the user to customize the layout more.

The best thing about free landscaping software is that it is free. It can usually be quickly and easily downloaded from the Internet, and if you find out that it is useless crippleware, then you can simply delete it and try another software package. It may take some time to find the one or ones that work for you, but you will not be out any cash in the process.

Most of this kind of free landscaping software will be easy to use and includes help files that give instructions. But since it is free software, there will rarely be any support available if you have a problem or question not covered in the help files.

HILLSIDE LANDSCAPING:
MAKE THAT HILL LOOK BEAUTIFUL!

If you live in a hilly area, you may have steep slopes in your yard. These can be a challenge to landscape, or even mow for fear of the lawn mower going out of control down the hill. But no matter how steep your hillsides are, you can do landscaping work on them.

One of the first things you should think about when considering a hillside landscaping project is safety. If you have a steep slope, you can easily fall down it yourself or send your equipment tumbling to the bottom. If you have very steep hills, it may be best to have professionals do the actual landscaping work, or at least terrace it so that you have flat areas to work in.

If the hill is not so steep, however, you can often do the landscaping yourself. begin by taking a good look at the land, its shape, and location. Make sure you take into account the overall flow of the land and its relationship with the rest of you property.

As an example, if the hillside is out in front of the house, you can create some very ornate approaches to your home. Check out the soil quality. Is it wet or dry? Sandy or clay? Just plain old dirt? Some amount of soil conditioning through the addition of good soil may be necessary for plants to thrive.

Try forgetting about small plants and plant some bushes instead. Bushes tend to be very hardy, and don't require too much pruning throughout most of the year. For a hillside landscaping project, you will probably want bushes that grow more horizontally than vertically.

Once you have chosen the types of bushes you want, you should design a pattern or layout to plant the bushes in. This may require some calculations on your part as you figure out where to place the bushes, how many you will need, and how much, if any, area needs to be dig out and flattened.

You can use a simple linear pattern, or get fancy with some curving lines. Try to make it all blend together well so that the overall effect is one of harmony. Discussing your ideas with a professional landscape designer can be a great help. If you get stuck, or just can't come up with any ideas you like, hiring one can be just the thing you need to get the project jump-started.

For more information and resources on hillside landscaping, check out the landscaping section and gardening magazines at your local bookstore. Your gardening center may also have some ideas, and can give advice on plants that do well in the local climate.

LANDSCAPING PICTURES OFFER DIFFERENT POSSIBILITIES

The extreme difficulty in trying to visualize exactly what your landscape could look like with some given changes can be helped some by examining landscaping pictures from homes of a similar design but different landscaping layouts. A lot of home improvement magazines, as well as gardening and landscaping publications, will have pictures that can be used for your own landscaping ideas.

Some drawbacks to trying to use landscaping pictures as a visualization and design aid is that you must carefully take into account key differences between your situation and that of the house being photographed. These pictures are usually taken under sunny blue skies with everything in full bloom. But that house may look completely different in the winter. It may also be in a completely different climate than yours, and often the plants you see in the landscaping pictures may not grow in your climate.

For this reason it is important that you be able to identify the various plants, shrubs, and flowers you will see in these landscaping pictures. Also beware of designs centering around a patio or porch that you may not have room to build. And be sure that you aren't planting things that will grow to be far too large for your yard.

Finding a house that closely resembles your can be a time consuming task. Really, the only way to do it is to sit down with a bunch of these publications and look through many landscaping pictures until you find ones that look similar to your house. Remember, that design that looks fantastic in a landscaping picture of a huge house may not look so nice crammed around a smaller house.

You will notice that a lot of the landscaping pictures you look at also include shots of pools and patios. Landscaping must be designed around this fixture, and if you do not have one, that layout will never look right in your yard. Landscaping pictures can give you some great ideas, but only if they house and yard resembles yours fairly closely.

If you are making use of some kind of landscaping software, you can print out landscaping pictures of your design once you have something you like. Taking these to a garden or landscaping supply shop can make sure that you have enough materials and plants to complete the project like you want. They may also be able to offer suggestions to improve your design.

LOW MAINTENANCE LANDSCAPING CHICAGO

People who live in the Chicago area and are interested in landscaping should keep some basic things in mind when designing their landscape. Use plants that are native to the Chicago area when possible. They are much easier to take care of since they are in their ideal climate. While working in your yard taking care of your plants may be fun at first, after a few years of caring for a yard full of high-maintenance plants you will be singing a different tune.

Chicago-native plants can be used to help take care of drainage problems you may have. Intelligent landscaping in Chicago can help alleviate the all-too-common drainage problems in the area. The weather can go through several different extreme over the course of a year, and this takes its toll on the soil. Always consider the weather before making any landscaping decisions in Chicago. If you are not sure, talk to a local landscaper about the plants suited for use in Chicago landscaping.

Don't skimp when you are putting your landscaping project together. People will be able to tell, and this can lead to hard feelings and embarrassment on your part. Take your time, there is no rush. Choose your plants and designs carefully, and always double-check to make sure that it is a viable setup. Take input, but realize that tastes differ, and what looks good to you may look horrible to another person, and the opposite is true.

When trying to choose plants for landscaping in Chicago, take a good look around you. What plants are your neighbors keeping? Which ones seem to be doing well, and which ones look like they are barely hanging on? Which ones look good to you? If you have hired a landscaper, not only should you talk to him about what the design should be, show him what plants and concepts you like and which one you do not. Any decent landscaper will try hard to design a landscape that you, the client, enjoy as priority number one.

When thinking about landscaping, Chicago perennials can be the best way to go. these plants come back on their own year after year, and can save you a whole lot of time, energy, and money from not having to plant new flowers every year. That can get old really quickly, especially if you are doing all the work yourself.

THE KEY TO LANDSCAPING DESIGN

If you are creating a landscape design and want it to be as good as it can be, you need to understand the concept of unity. This is absolutely key to a good landscape design and needs to be applied to your entire yard and home exterior. A balanced look and feel is what you are striving for, with a sense of continuity to all landscape design elements.

You can achieve this feeling of wholeness in your landscape design in several different ways. The most basic thing to start with is using the similar kinds of trees and plants throughout your design. This is one of the easier things you can do for your landscape design, and will look excellent if some thought is put into it.

Being aware of and using heights to your advantage is another key concept. Use trees of similar heights, and plants and shrubs of similar heights as well. This can bring a feeling of completeness and wholeness to your landscape design.

But any good landscape design uses many more elements than only plants and trees. Flowers are beautiful, and con provide needed color and accents, they only bloom for a part of the year (unless you are lucky enough to live in a tropical climate). This means you need to find other elements to balance your landscape design out year round. Rocks and landscaping stones can be used to great effect, and wood chips can provide an interesting base for your plants. If you have a larger budget, using stone such as granite or marble can create wonderful effects in your landscape design. Stepping stones, statues, and fountains are just a few more elements that can be considered in addition to the plants.

Having some sort of theme in mind can help out a lot when attempting to achieve a unified landscape design. If you want lots of butterflies or birds, for instance, choose plants and settings that will attract them into your yard. The presence of these living creatures can provide that final touch that takes your landscape design from good to great.

When it is all said and done, your landscape design should have a flow and sense of continuity from the beginning of your yard to the end. And remember, your landscape design is for you above all else. if you like it, don't let someone else tell you that it is not good enough.

WHAT DOES YOUR LANDSCAPING PLAN NEED?

There are several things a landscaping plan will need to be a successful one. First of all, you need to understand what makes a good landscaping plan in the first place. To work, a landscaping plan must be well thought out, and any potential issues dealt with. this means taking such things as the amount of sun a part of your yard receives each day, how much water it will receive and if more may be needed, and drainage into consideration before you start working on your landscaping plan. Drainage and irrigation both are very important issues that must be dealt with for a thriving yard to be created.

You should take a close look at all the existing elements of your yard before embarking on a landscaping plan. The best landscaping plans make use of natural features and plants that are already there in your yard. Don't cut down that huge old oak tree, for example. Design around it and your landscaping plan will look much better overall. there may be interesting terrain features that can be incorporated. there is no reason to completely tear out your yard before landscaping it. Everything will look much more natural and beautiful if you work with nature, not against it.

After taking a good look around, start thinking about any major terrain changes or dirt work that may need to be done. Do you need to build up that hill over there, or level it? How about the shape and flow of your yard? is it good, or could it use a little bit of reshaping? All these things are important parts of your landscaping plan.

Most of the time, you won't have millions of dollars to spare on landscaping, so any plan you make should take into account your budget. Getting some prices on the various elements that will be used in your landscaping plan can help you see what you can and can't afford to do.

Terrain work especially is expensive and disruptive. Don't try to completely reshape your yards elevations, as the cost will likely be prohibitive.

Take you time when coming up with a landscaping plan, try to take all factors into account, and only after you are sure that you have a plan that you are comfortable with and that is complete should you start any of the actual work on the landscaping project.

NOT ALL LANDSCAPING SOFTWARE
IS CREATED EQUAL

While there are some absolutely fantastic landscaping software packages out there that can take you from bare dirt to a finished landscape plan, there are others out there that are a total waste of money and time. The trick lies in figuring out which landscaping software is good and which to avoid.

A lot of the landscaping software packages on the market that re aimed at the average consumer are really not very good. Some of these consumer packages can be absolutely awful, and buying them is about as good as throwing money into the fireplace. They will have a horrible amateur look and feel to them, with cartoonish interfaces and low-quality graphics output. The more expensive commercial packages made for professional landscape designers can totally blow you away with the output quality and features they can provide.

The biggest thing most people forget is that landscaping software of any kind is only a tool. There is no such thing as landscaping software that can create your landscape entire without user input. They are only tools to help you better visualize and plan your landscaping project. The actual work still has to be done to make your dream a reality. If you are trying to purchase landscaping software thinking it will do everything for you, you are going to be wasting your money.

Before you decide on a particular landscaping software package to purchase, you should always get a demo. Any serious package is going to have a demo available, because these software companies realize that people are not going to spend big bucks on software that they have never tried out. When checking out various landscaping software, try and stick to the ones with good graphics. A primitive, cartoon-like visualization of your landscape ideas are not going to help you. You need clear, sharp, and above all, realistic graphics to really get the full benefit of these landscaping software packages.

Getting demos and trying out various programs can give you a much better idea of which landscaping software will be able to meet your needs, and which ones are just a waste of your money. This bears repeating: If a software company does not have some kind of demo available that you can try out, their product is often not worth even considering for purchase. The more expensive landscaping software may not have a demo posted for just anyone to download, but demos of this landscaping software can be had by contacting the company and asking for a demo in most cases.

DO YOU KNOW HOW TO CHOOSE
THE RIGHT LANDSCAPING SUPPLY STORE?

When you are about to start a landscaping project, picking the right landscape supply store can make a huge difference to your bottom line. You can't approach this like a normal consumer; rather, approach finding a supplier for your landscape project like you are doing a huge job and need to save money where possible. There are quite a few landscape supply stores out there, but only a few are worth dealing with, and they aren't the ones you see advertising sales on TV.

The landscape supply stores you are looking for are the ones that cater to people who work in the landscaping industry. These landscape supply stores sell their products at an often hefty chunk below retail, but still above wholesale. If you can manage to both find them and convince them to sell to you, you can save a ton of money on your landscaping project. This can be difficult, however, as many of these stores do not like to deal with the general public.

Try talking to some professional landscapers and see if you can pry some information about their suppliers out of them. They will often be reluctant to divulge this information, but with patience, persistence, and a little bit of luck you can find out where the landscape supply stores you are looking for are. Then go to this store and see if they will actually sell to you. A lot of stores that cater to the professionals are not usually open for sales to the general public.

If you don't have any success in getting a contractor to tell you where the good suppliers are, you can always go through the phone book and look for landscape supply stores that way. Try checking different categories if you are not having any luck with the one you are searching under. Basically, do whatever you have to find out where the professionals are getting their landscaping supplies from. They all have to buy from somewhere, and no self-respecting contractor pays retail for his materials, so they have to be getting it from somewhere. The money saved in the long run by finding the right landscape supply store is well worth the hassle of finding it in the first place.

POOL LANDSCAPING WILL REQUIRE SIGNIFICANT THOUGHT

Whether you are considering adding a pool into your existing landscaping, adding landscaping around an existing pool, or starting completely from scratch, there are some special considerations that must be addressed before starting a project like this. Choosing the plants the will be used is an important part of this process.

The choice of plants will depend on your pool, location, existing landscaping, and other factors. If you pool is above ground, you would use completely different plants than you would for below ground pool landscaping. In particular, trees, shrubs, and even smaller plants should all be kept away from an in ground pool, as the roots can grow through and crack the concrete, leading to a leaking in ground pool that is a bear to fix. Most in ground pools will have a privacy fence of some sort, and plants and trees should be chosen and placed outside of this perimeter. Some plants can be used in open spots inside this fence, but again, keep them well clear of the pool itself.

For indoor pools, plants should probably be some variety of evergreens, since the leaves off of deciduous plants can collect in the pool. Even some evergreens, especially the kind with needles, can get leaves into the pool and possible clog the filters. Any plants placed near the pool should be as simple and hardy as possible. Most annual flowers and plants cannot stand exposure to pool water, due to the chlorine in it. Creeping vines of any kind should also be avoided, as they can cause the same problems as tree roots, combined with a tendency to take over any open surface area they can reach.

Outside the fence, you are afforded much more flexibility when choosing your plants, but remember that more flowers and annuals, while often very pretty, require much more work to maintain and replant every year. Try to avoid plants that will grow higher than the fence surrounding the pool, as their leaves will wind up in your pool if they are growing over the fence.

Small clusters of short flowers placed in strategic locations can really liven up your pool landscaping without adding an undue amount of extra work to take care of them. Shrubs can contribute to the apparent height of a fence, but should be kept trimmed below the top of the fence. And don't forget that certain flowers and plants can attract flying insects that may not be desirable and can interrupt you and your guests' enjoyment of the pool if they are particular nuisances.

GARDENING TIPS:
GROWING HOT PEPPERS

Hot peppers are found all over the world, but primarily in hot climates such as Mexico and Southeast Asia. Many hot peppers are also cultivated in green or hot houses, which are simply regulated and contained environments. Hot peppers are found all over the world, and have been adding spice to meals for centuries. The hotter the pepper, the more capsaicinoids it has. Capsaicinoids are what cause the burning feeling when you eat a very hot pepper. The higher the capsaicinoid content the more intensely you will feel the burn. The Scoville Scale is used to measure how hot a pepper is in Scoville units. The Scoville Scale was developed in 1912 by Wilbur Scoville. Since then the method for determining Scoville units in hot pepper has become much more scientific (no more taste tests).

Once you know the Scoville rating of a hot pepper you can get a good idea how hot it will be and how to use it in your cooking without causing yourself unnecessary discomfort. Pure capsaicin has a rating of 16,000,000, whereas a bell pepper has a rating of 0. One of the most popular moderately hot peppers is the jalapeno, which has a rating of anywhere between 2,500 and 8,000 Scoville units. Compare this with varieties of habanero peppers which come in anywhere from 100,000 to 300.000 Scoville units. Some other highly rating hot peppers include Scotch bonnet peppers and Jamaican hot peppers. Due to the vast difference between peppers, it is wise to never substitute a pepper in a recipe for another unless you know they have similar Scoville ratings.

Many people love to grow their own hot peppers and in the right environment you may find they grow quicker than you can eat them. You can grow hot peppers in your garden, or even in containers. If you are a novice gardener you may want to start with plants rather than seeds.

Each pepper plant or seed packet should come with very specific instructions on planting, watering, and sunlight. Most hot pepper varieties require at least five hours of direct sunlight a day, and moist but not drenched soil. Adding some plant food to the soil is a great way to encourage healthy large hot peppers. Before planting peppers make sure that the environment in which you live will get hot enough to produce a healthy pepper plant. Some cooler climates may not be ideal for the pepper plant and the seeds and seedlings may need to be cultured indoors before turning out into the garden.

GARDENING TIPS: STARTING A BUTTERFLY GARDEN

There are hundreds upon hundreds of species of butterflies. In Los Angeles California alone there are over 110 different species. In New York City there are about 70 different species. So of course there are going to be people like you who'd like to enjoy seeing some of these species within their own gardens and that's where this article comes in handy. Butterflies are beautiful and it's always a nice surprise to see them flitting about, in and out of flowers unexpectedly. So why not have them in your personal garden as well? There are plenty of things you can do to attract different types of butterflies to your garden. You don't need a special garden all by itself to attract butterflies. If you have certain plants and flowers in the garden, butterflies will definitely find them.

First of all you should know that some plants that attract butterflies can also attract bees and wasps. So if you have allergies to these bugs or just don't want them hanging around then you might want to rethink the whole butterfly garden thing. Once you get past that you need to choose flowers and plants that butterflies love, places for them to sun themselves, and a supply of water somewhere in the garden for them to drink. It should be a place that not only the adults are attracted to but should be a place for them to hibernate, lay eggs, and for the larva and caterpillars to feed. You should create a place to hibernate that is protected in some way, like with surrounding tall trees that help as a barrier from wind. They like to bask in the warm sun so why not have flat rocks about just for that purpose.

Butterflies are mostly active in mid and late summer so you should make sure that you have lots of nectar-rich plants and flowers blooming by then. If you plant large sections of flowers that are the same color it'll make it easier for them to find you garden. You should plant flowers that will bloom at different times of the year and ones that bloom even at different times of the day and night, this way you'll always have something in bloom and they'll always be attracting butterflies.

Once you find out which types of butterflies are native to your area, it'll be easier to know which kinds of plants and flowers to put in your garden. Don't forget though, that you should alternate your "butterfly plants and flowers" with ones that don't attract butterflies also. If you actually have so many butterflies in your garden, you can place water features and "calm" areas also. Having an entire garden dedicated to butterflies isn't necessary either. If you'd like, you can have a mini butterfly garden by adding a raised section to your garden and then that's where you'd plant everything.

GARDENING TIPS: COMPOST

Healthy compost is essential for any garden whether you're growing vegetables or flowers. Compost is essentially organic decaying matter. Aerobic organisms such as insects, bacteria, fungi, and worms break down materials such as grass, leaves, and some kitchen scraps to create compost. Compost is extremely rich in nutrients and comparable, if not better, than commercial fertilizers for your garden. Many gardeners use compost since it is free, environmentally friendly, and wonderful for your plants. If you're able to save your kitchen scraps you might want to take advantage of producing your own compost.

There is almost no limit to the many benefits of compost. Rich in nitrogen, phosphorus, and potassium compost is sure to help any garden become abundant. Compost improves soil and encourages root development. Any gardener who has used compost is sure to never go back to commercial fertilizer. After just a short time of using home made compost you'll start to notice the difference in the way your plants are thriving.

If you are interested in composting you do need a compost bin. Some people still have a traditional compost bin, which is an open bin of any sort, typically wood, which they throw compost materials into. The composting process can however take some time and the new and improved compost bins take advantage of what we know about heat and moisture conditions.

Anyone can have a compost bin, even if you have a very small yard or live in an apartment with a large balcony.

Compost materials are the matter that you place inside your compost bin and will eventually become your compost for gardening. Almost any organic matter will do and they typically fall into two groups: brown and green materials. Matter rich in carbon are considered browns and include dried leaves and straw. Matter rich in nitrogen are considered greens and include certain kitchen scraps such as vegetables and fruits and grass. As you can see compost materials are very easy to come by since any home owner has an abundance of these materials.

Other than your garden, one of the biggest benefits to composting is the environment. In this day and age where everything is disposable and our landfills are growing by the second, it is important we do what we can to help reduce and reuse. Composting is a wonderful way to do your part by reducing the amount of garbage we throw away and reusing certain materials.

Composting is essentially recycling waste and turning it into something our gardens will love.

GARDENING TIPS:
ORGANIC GARDENING

Organic gardening means that you need to know a whole range of tips and tricks so that you can have a successful garden. When you have the knowledge, the tips, and the patience to garden naturally you've got a recipe for success. You'll find yourself with a beautiful flower garden and baskets of fresh vegetables with no more effort or time that you would invest in a garden that isn't taken care of organically.

Mulching is an important step for any type of garden. You'll have to use organic mulch in your flower and vegetable gardens so this means that you may want to make your own mulch from ingredients from your own home. Mulching will add nutrition to the soil, helps combat weeds, and acts as a water retainer. For those plants that you have that need to have an acid mulch, all you need to do is add a sprinkling of pine needles to the mulched area and this will naturally elevate the acid content of the soil.

If you're going to garden organically you'll have to make sure that any fertilizers that you buy are natural and organic. You'll be able to find organic fertilizers in plant and gardening stores as well as other organic supplements that you may want to add to the soil. Pests, such as insects, are always a big concern for the organic gardener. Inviting birds to your yard by hanging bird feeders are one way that you can keep down the number of insects that you have in your garden. Keep in mind though that there are some birds that will love to eat the tender shoots of your plants. For example, sparrows love to eat parsley, radish tops, and new lettuce so you'll want to try to avoid luring these birds to the bird feeder.

There are other ways that you can get rid of the bugs and pests that are out to eat your plants besides luring birds or using pesticides. You can get rid of the aphids on your plants by spraying the stems, leaves, and buds with a solution that has been made of soap and water. It's important that you remember to spray the soap solution into the dirt around and near the stems of the plants so that you further deter the aphids from eating the plant.

You can find many books on organic gardening to give you more hints and tips about how to keep your garden growing and flourishing. You'll soon enjoy eating organic vegetables and having a flower garden that is totally free of chemicals.

GARDENING TIPS:
PATIO GARDENING

If you have a green thumb you may have beautiful landscaping, a vegetable plot, and houseplants. Or, you may love plants but don't have the luxury of a big backyard or your health may prevent large-scale gardening. This is when it's time to turn to that empty patio or balcony for gardening possibilities. A patio is an oft-neglected space that homeowners or apartment renters forget to use so why not perk it up with plants? The benefits are many, and the convenience can't be beat!

A trellis with ivy or other climbing plants can be the best way to shield you from neighbors' nosy gazes. Trellises can also provide reprieve from unsightly back yards or a noisy street. If the idea of a trellis doesn't appeal, you can always place a hearty ficus or other large container plant to obscure the view off your patio or balcony. A wooden deck, concrete patio, or iron balcony are negative spaces that become inviting when decorated with plants. Hanging plants, like spider plants or ferns, can make a space cozier when you sit on a swing or bench in cool evenings, giving the impression that you and your guests are "peeking" out into the view. Small, hearty outdoor plants are great placed on a tiered stand or on the railing, providing visual interest.

Vegetables, like cherry tomatoes or lemon trees, can make having fresh produce right at your fingertips possible. There are many vegetables and fruits that do well in pots. This is great for gardeners with limited space or mobility. Herbs are also a nice addition to your patio garden, as they are beautiful as well as useful. Patio gardens can be as large or small as your taste or space permits. You may prefer a southwestern look with lots of cacti. Maybe you want the lush appearance of leafy green plants and blooming flowers. A minimalist may want to keep his or her patio garden limited to a lemon tree and a pot of Asian grasses.

Also remember that the pots themselves can serve as decorative focal points. These you can buy new in complementary colors, find at flea markets for an eclectic look, or paint yourself. If you want the plants themselves to be the star of the show use simple terra cotta pots. For green plants, colored pots are often attractive. It's also possible to match the pot to the flower color. For example, a lavender plant would be beautiful in a shiny periwinkle bowl.

Finally, patio gardens are easy to tend to. Plants can be moved around for best light and moved indoors in the colder months. Watering is small-scale with a household watering can. The only tool necessary is a small garden spade. With a weekly tour, patio gardens can be kept neat looking with a pair of scissors and broom. If you haven't got the space, the energy, or the time for a full-size garden, but still want to experience the serenity and beauty they bring, turn to your patio into your haven. Convenient and beautiful, patio gardens are gardens at you fingertips.

GARDENING TIPS: WINTER GARDENING

The temperatures are slowly declining, the trees are becoming bare, and the weatherman is predicting the first frost of the season. Surely the winter season holds no hope of producing a garden full of healthy plants, right? Wrong! There are several things you can do to extend the period of time during which you can plant a successful garden. The winter even provides some benefits such as natural pest control, which will help your garden reach its maximum potential. In addition, by carefully choosing plants that are durable and frost-resistant you can ensure that they will survive through some undesirable conditions and be ready for harvest in the late fall or even mid-winter.

It's probably a good idea to sit down and start planning out all of the aspects of your garden on paper, to provide you with a solid blueprint you can reference when it comes time to purchase supplies and start doing the dirty work. The types of plants you choose to grow will affect most of the other decisions you will need to make about your garden, so it is advisable to take care of this first. There are many types of vegetables that will suit your needs for a fall and winter garden. Some of the more popular ones include lettuce, broccoli, carrots, cabbage, onions, spinach, and turnips. All of these vegetables have been known to be frost-resistant, and therefore make perfect candidates for the garden.

Once you've decided what types of plants you want head over to the local nursery to purchase some seed packets of the vegetables you want to grow. Make sure to take a look at the number of days required for them to mature. This information is usually found on the packet itself.

Once you've got the number of days simply backtrack from the projected date for your region's first frost, and plant the seeds. Your garden should already be prepared for its new inhabitants that mean replacing the nutrient-depleted soil from your spring garden if necessary. Soil drainage must be excellent in the wintertime. If the water cannot pass through the soil, it will freeze and damage your plant's roots. If you are concerned about drainage in your garden, adding sand can improve the situation.

When planting the seeds, make sure you are giving the plants more room than you would normally. This will improve air circulation and ensure that fungus and mildew won't be taking advantage of any dark, damp places you've unintentionally created by sticking your plants too close to each other.

Successful gardening in the winter is all about planning and protection. If you've chosen plants that are durable and frost-resistant, you've already got an advantage. By carefully planning out your garden, you can improve air circulation and prevent harmful fungus or other pests from finding a home with your plants. Basic protective layers will help your plants survive unusually cold, frosty nights. Follow these basic guidelines and you should be able to enjoy your garden all year round!

GARDENING TIPS:
CREATING A WILDLIFE GARDEN

Many people opt for a natural garden because of the enjoyment derived from the various specimens of wildlife that visit. Another appreciated attribute is low maintenance. The less you maintain your garden, the greater diversity you encourage. These gardens work with, and benefit from, nature and wildlife. Other garden types can also benefit from nature and wildlife. Your garden soil, plants growing in it, and natural debris on its surface abound with a multitude of various organisms. Though some are invisible to the human eye they have a profound affect on the lives of plants and animals, large and small. They are an important part of the biological community, helping to provide food for animals and birds.

A wise gardener will support these microorganisms by providing them with plenty of organic matter to recycle. The caregiver of a natural garden is one such gardener, and understands the benefits of working side by side with nature. Whether a natural garden or not, there are good, viable reasons for encouraging certain specimens of wildlife to the garden. Toads and frogs help to control garden pests and ladybugs have voracious appetites when it comes to aphids. Worms help to aerate the soil, praying mantis seek out a variety of "bad insects," and butterflies and bees help pollinate. But there are many other reasons to encourage wildlife interaction in the garden.

Besides being a delight to watch birds are useful in the yard and garden because they eat a large variety and quantity of insects. Swallows eat their weight in insects each day, including pesky mosquitoes. Robins, flycatchers, vireos, warblers, and woodpeckers are also primarily insect eaters. Even hummingbirds will occasionally supplement their diet of flower nectar with insects. In fact, birds are among the best natural means of keeping garden pests in check. In order to encourage birds to your yard and garden a few basic needs must be met: food, water, shelter, and a place to rear young. A wise gardener will provide an environment that will offer birds these basic needs.

Water should be made available during every season of the year. During winters in northern states or in the mountains, where hard freezes occur, a small immersed heater made for that purpose will keep a pond or birdbath from icing over. You can help insure that birds will visit often by providing bird feeders in and around your yard. To attract a wide variety of birds, offer a variety of feeding stations and different types of food. If hawks are prevalent in your area, shelter these feeding stations with a wire roof. Birds will be better protected against predators, and you will still be able to see and enjoy them.

GARDENING TIPS: COMMON PESTS

There are many ways to protect your lawn, flowers, vegetables and trees against tiny predators that are historically safe and efficient. Aphids are small, soft-bodied threats to foliage; these pests suck your plant's sap and cause the plant to wither. Worse, aphids carry and transmit disease and are of particular concern for tomato plants. You can control them from wreaking extensive damage to your garden by introducing ladybugs to the organic arena. You can buy ladybugs from many different suppliers. The apple maggot, similar to the common housefly, is also known as a railroad worm and apple fruit fly. Whatever you name it, it is responsible for messy pulpy apples. One way to thwart these creatures is to hang plastic fruit coated with Tanglefoot that will render useless the feet of the insect keeping them from your rosy apples.

Protect your beans from bean thrip that are dark thin pests that leave plants leaves wilted and visibly spotted with excrement. To keep their population under control keep your garden as free from weeds as possible. Also, try incorporating lacewings, bugs that prey on thrips. A major enemy of cabbage and its relatives is the harlequin bug. This is a black bug with red-orange markings that smells horrible. It also causes the plant to wilt and turn brown.

You'll need a decoy crop of mustard greens nearby to lure these smelly pests over. Remove the bugs here and drop them in a jar of kerosene-topped water.

Vegetable weevils attack many kinds of veggies such as cabbage, carrots and cauliflower. You can best control them by rotating your crops. The cultivation should destroy their underground eggs. Serious pests for your lawn are chinch bugs. Introduce bigeyed bugs to munch down their numbers and keep your grass looking green and healthy. Cutworms will threaten your carnation population, but they will threaten just about everything else in your garden too. Luckily, many predators find this ghastly looking creature appetizing including fireflies, meadowlarks, and toads among them.

A garden hose is a good way to protect your evergreens from spider mites. If you see yellow needles there is good chance you've got them. A forceful blast from the hose up and down the center of the tree periodically will help wash them away. A water spray is an effective way to rid many plants, such as your English ivy, from various mites. A small squirt can wash the creature and its web away. Many insects can be controlled and stopped simply by keeping your garden free of weeds that attract and shelter the pests.

GARDENING TIPS: TYPES OF SOIL

Dirt is actually not the correct term to describe that complex growing media that plants need to…well…grow. Soil is composed of bacteria and microorganisms that help decompose organic matter into nutrients that enrich the soil. As gardeners will tell some soils are better than others for growing various different types of plants. Depending on your conditions your garden soil might need some help.

Clay soil is known as a heavy soil. When wet its particles clump together making it impervious to both water and plants. When clay soil becomes dry it stays hard and cracks. Consequently clay soil delights in air and the soil needs to be loosened. Most gardeners will add peat moss or humus to their clay soil in order to prevent the particles from sticking together and will allow water to drain through it. Sandy soils are composed of the largest particles found in soils.

Sandy soil has such excellent drainage that often its problem is an inability to retain moisture for good plant growth. Again, humus or peat moss can remedy this situation.

A silt soil is generally a good growing soil since its particles are in sizes between those of clay and sand. A loam soil is usually excellent for plants. It is open, retains moisture well and has a good structure. Loam is the gardener's joy. Other types of growing soil can be purchased online or at your local garden center. Humus is basically composted topsoil. It is rich with decomposed organic matter and is sold much like regular topsoil. Generally humus can be purchased as peat humus or pine bark humus. The peat humus variety is mostly comprised of decomposed reed-sedge. Pine bark humus comes from decomposed pine bark. Humus is generally used to build up the soil structure for containers, lawns and flowerbeds.

Potting soil is sold for ready use. Also known as houseplant soil it is perfect for indoor plants and for starting plants from seed. Potting soil is a compound of both organic and inorganic materials with such ingredients as compost, peat moss, sand, and vermiculite. Top soil is rich with a large quantity of organic composition. Most gardeners turn to packaged topsoil from one time to another to improve the quality of their garden soil. It can be purchased sterile or in its natural form containing microorganisms. Soilless mixes are sold for use in container or tub gardens. These have been sterilized so there is no likelihood of weeds. This growing medium retains water and nutrients extremely well.

These are most of the basics when it comes to soil. There are more soil conditioners and additives on the market but you will need to know what your garden soil needs for plants to thrive. In some cases, a soil test for pH levels is ideal for determining the components of your garden soil. There are test kits available. Check online or at your local garden center.

GARDENING TIPS:
STARTING WITH A NEW GARDEN

It's that time of the year again where you might feel like you could really try to start your own garden again. Whether your heart lies with growing vegetables, flowers, or just designing and maintaining a gorgeous garden you have to start somewhere. There is nothing more fulfilling than growing your plants and vegetables from seed especially if you are interested in starting an organic garden. Organic seeds for both plants and vegetables or fruits are widely available nowadays and there are always people who would gladly swap seeds. Giving your plants the right start is imperative when it comes to growing strong plants and sowing and growing from seed is an art in itself. It will take a bit more work and determination but seeing a plant develop in its own time is an educational and exciting thing to witness.

Growing indoors in heated propagators sold in any garden centre or just on the window sill can be done all year round. Growing outdoors is where the true challenge lies. Be prepared to guard your young plant against pests such as slugs and follow these steps to a successful garden. Start by forking over the soil of the chosen site where you wish to start your garden a few times before you actually start sowing. This is done to encourage the growth of weeds before you sow so that you can successfully hoe off the weed seedlings. The traditional time to start this process would be February or March. Shortly before you start sowing all the weeds must have been removed.

Pick a dry day and make sure that the soil that you will be working with is not wet. Scatter a fertilizer suitable for the type of garden that you are preparing over the ground. This could be organic compost suitable for vegetables for example. Your garden centre will be able to help you find the best fertilizer for your plot or garden. After this process the ground must be raked over and over again till it is completely level, to make sowing easier.

Early in the season the soil might still be fairly damp and cold. If this is the case it might be wise to first cover the prepared soil with sheets of plastic for a few weeks or so, till you are satisfied that the weather has made a change for the better and there will be no more spells of frost. The plastic will help warm the soil and the top layer of the soil will dry out a bit, which will make sowing a lot easier when you can start. If you cannot wait it might be an idea to construct a tunnel of plastic with plastic piping, to sow and grow seedling under.

FLORIST – USE THEM FOR THE FLORAL/ FLOWER GARDENING IDEA

Apart from just looking pretty within your garden, flowers could be gathered and shaped into various gorgeous arrangements for many special occasions, or simply to decorate your house. One may obviously do this individually; however there are some people who are trained in this art of flower arrangement which you could turn to formal arrangements and some tips on arranging one's own flowers. The expert individuals are the florists. The floral/flower gardening fountain of knowledge always waits to be tapped.

Due to the fact that several florists arrange the flowers according to different themes, you could always pop into some florist shop for an idea of what could be planted if one wants to make most out of the chosen flowers for the garden. Even before one chooses the flowers, it is suggested to go on idea hunting by entering your local florist shop. Floral/flower gardening and suggestions would be abound.

You could turn towards some florist for the flower gardening tips or other information about growing flowers. If one is actually lucky, the florist would be growing his own stock and hence could take you around the garden to show about how specific flowers are precisely taken care of.

Some traditional florists who are specialized in selling exotic flower arrangements, also occasionally sell some species of flowers and the seedlings which you may then transplant in the garden. Few traditional florists do not sell the seeds; however, besides transplanting flowers which are bought from the florist shop, one could buy flowers and take the cutting to cultivate one's own specimen of the flower.

These days, moreover, the garden supplies store and other supermarkets are getting into florist business. They would always remain the reliable locations from where one could buy the gardening plants and other garden supplies; however, now one may head to most of such places for really stunning floral arrangements.

In the technology era, apparently there are several places for virtual florists. The floral/flower gardening companies are not just the only ones jumping in the World Wide Web. Quite many of the florists are heavily popping up on internet sites. They are very convenient as one may have the flowers sent to any corner in the world. If in case whatever you are looking in the florist is more of personal attention and a possibility about walking through a shop taking look at the floral arrangements for the inspiration, then the online florists would just not do.

Indeed, one cannot just choose a florist for either the floral arrangements or regarding any advice on flower growing. Ensure that the florist you plan to turn to is very creative in his work. This would help you with getting wonderful advices on what could be essentially grown! The manner in which the florist asks you about your purpose of growing and wanting the flowers is another sign of good florist etiquette. Floral/flower gardening tips which are from such people could be trusted. They would indeed give tailored and personal advice. Always check the selection of the flowers which are offered by florists. The floral/flower gardening advice must only be heard from people who have several different species in their shop as these florists have wider range of information and knowledge and would give more extensive advice. Always beware of those florists who sell fewer flower species as their knowledge is very limited. Lastly, ensure that the flowers which are being sold stay in good shape. It would suggest that the florist is one who knows to care about the flowers and could pass on that information to you.

INDOOR GARDENING SUPPLIES FOR WINTER FUN

Which gardener would not sit inside in winter with some plant catalogues on their lap as they sip their tea and dream of the next year's garden? This is simply a good fun especially to get indoor gardening supply and have a little winter gardening fun. You may use it for starting seedlings or simply raise indoor plants; however either way with right indoor gardening supply, one need not wait for the summer to get his fingers dirty again.

Light- let that remain

Perhaps, the most vital thing to address about indoor gardening is regarding the level of light. During the winters, days are shorter which means less light. When the house does not have suitable windows facing south to capture good light, you would continually have to append the light quotient by adjusting the plants around for capturing better sun. It is not optimal solution though. For the winter indoor gardening, apt light sources are among the essential indoor gardening supply stuff. Few people rely upon fluorescent lights, and some others use halogen lights and high intensity discharge lamps. Few even try growing them with the incandescent light, but it doesn't work very well for every plant.

Any way for that matter, one must be aware about the light requirements of indoor plants which is being grown and should pick the lighting suitable for them.

Earth or Water

There is varied number of ways you could grow plants inside, few are based on the nutrients rich water-based system, and some others rely upon the good Mother Earth. Type of garden chosen would determine indoor gardening supplies one needs. The soil-less systems, generally called the hydroponics are considered as optimal indoor growing system. It reduces damage to the crops from pests and weeds. It is a little more complex to comprehend, but could be learned quite quickly. The indoor gardening supplies often have assortments of hydroponics kits which are available to average consumer.

When you are rooting the cuttings or growing the seeds for transplanting outdoor, then the jiffy peat cups and seedling starter kits become available in the indoor gardening supplies. It would allow you to plant the seeds indoors with minimum mess via soil. They are compact, very easily transported, and peat pots could be planted outside pot!

Indoor gardening is indeed a rewarding hobby. Most people focus on specific plant types. Few like cactuses, while others like tropical. Some other people grow the herbs indoors. Whichever plant you choose, it would have its very own unique growing needs and other optimal environments. Cactuses, apparently, would need a very dry and hot environment whereas the herbs love the hydroponic setups. Hence when you choose the indoor gardening supplies, always ensure about the plants you would grow and try mimicking the environment in which they essentially grow naturally for best results.

CAST IRON FURNITURE

Cast iron furniture would add a good element of beauty in people's patio and garden. Nothing exists like exclusive state of art process about manufacturing the furniture which is cast iron. The beautiful patio would add the required beauty and grace to anyone's house. Most families live on patio in the long hot months of summer. Garden Furniture gets huge importance like those of household furnishings. This furniture must remain comfortable, easy to keep clean, fit all family needs, and must be affordable.

Possibly one may have never thought about cast iron furniture for the patio; however, this is a remarkable way of beautifying your patio. Such cast iron furniture seems to be inexpensive, more lasting and very comfortable. People today are introduced to Thermosint(c) Process that is used by the Contract Furniture Company for making cast iron furniture. Such cast iron is initially welded and sanded. Then the bare metal frame undergoes PH balance wash and a primer coating process. It is an important step in crafting cast iron to beautiful designs for furniture.

Then comes the premièred frame which is heated at about 660 degrees Fahrenheit in Thermal Tunnel before dipping it in the air injected powdered mixture of paint. Air-circulated powder, which consists of the paint pigments, the aluminum flakes and the resin particles, ensures even bonding of the frame, building up towards eight miles of paint.

With outer shell remaining uncured, the coated frame enters thermal tunnel again for the final heating process that is at about 390 degrees Fahrenheit. Paint is totally dried and hardened creating company's one of the kind finish which is nearly eight times thicker compared to standard powder coat. It is approximately fifteen times more thickly compared to a wet coat. The Contract Furniture Company's state of the art exclusive process ensures to resist scratching, fading, peeling, or chipping. Moreover, frame remains about fifty percent cooler when touched even long after it is exposed to sunlight. Company offers about 5 years of anti-rust guarantee that farther reassures about the cast iron furniture meeting the best standards among different furniture artisanship. The important parts are trademarks of Contract Furniture Company with none of the cast iron company using such specific procedures.

We can review the 4 elements in Contract Furniture Company; the metal finishing:

1. The iron profile or the solid iron as one permanent, stable and structural materials.

2. The iron phosphate undercoat for increasing the bonding and protection from rust.

3. A Primer coat for the improved and even bonding of the sintered coating.

4. Thermosint(c) is up to 8 times stronger when compared to standard powder coating of varnish.

We can explain why Contract Furniture Company; The Thermosint(c) is best.

1) Five years of anti-rust guarantee assurance.

2) Remains 50 percent cooler to the touch even after continuous exposure to sun.

3) 8 times thickly when compared to a standard coating.

4) 15 times more thicker when compared to the standard wet coating.

5) Extremely smooth finishing and the weld points are obsolete.

96

6) It assists in resisting scratching, fading, peeling, and chipping.

As it is apparent about how the craftsmen in Contract Furniture Company design the Cast Iron Outdoor Furniture, one must visit their showroom to see the exquisite pieces created.

GARDENING CATALOG

Gardening catalogue is an excellent entity for gardeners when they purchase things their heart desires. They can get anything the garden needs without leaving the house. The gardening catalogues would offer wider varieties at cheaper rates with fewer hassles involved. One may order things they want and have it delivered to the door; ready to use.

These catalogues are treasure troves of information for beginners and experienced gardeners. They would give detailed description about the plant types present for purchase, the growing and blooming season, and the maintenance which is involved. They would tell readers precisely about the nutrients which each plant needs and proper times for administering them.

Catalogues give tips and various hints on things like controlling weeds and diseases which may infect the plants. Step-by-step planting instructions are given, such as the amount of sunlight needed, and the seasons best for the planting times.

This would be kept in mind and catalogues would wait and then ship these goods so that they are received at the right planting time according to the zone one lives in.

The gardening catalogues would have all the equipment one could possibly require for almost any kind of gardening. If there is a hydroponics garden, timed water pump could be ordered or things like the artificial lighting. You may order pruning shears for the shrubs or some gas operated tiller for breaking up the dirt. Catalogues would give a larger selection of gloves, for making it possible about finding pair which is operational and also fashionable. Some other tools which could be purchased include hoes, rakes, spades, water hoses, shovels and the sprinklers. It is however not limited to them.

Gardening catalogues give the gardeners to choose from a wide selection of seeds and the plant variants which could be found elsewhere. The plus-point about catalogues is all things being offered at once. One could look through things available and then pick choosing ones which you wish planting based on requirements, like the maintenance of plants, time, and climatic needs. Gardening catalogue would give the luxury of knowing every plant type at once, making it easier to lay the choice.

These catalogues, above everything else, are very convenient. If one does not stay near the nursery or any gardening store, it would be difficult to search all things needed to initiate and maintain a healthy garden. It should be faced practically; Wal-Mart doesn't have everything needed for a garden. The gardening catalogues give more options allowing viewing things available on single settings. No matter whether one is in the market for equipment or seeds; a gardening catalogue would be the best way to go.

GARDENING

One thing to keep in mind during gardening is starting it small. Small plant bed which is about 25 to 30 feet square is quite perfect. It is aptly enough room for around 30 plants. This would give a chance for trying out the green thumb. If one finds it like enjoying the garden then they could always expand increasing the plantings.

Immediate next thing one would want to do would be choosing a site. The gardening activity must be done in areas which gets around six hours of good sunlight. One must try to stay away from big trees which might take the plants water and other nutrients. They must be at least about three feet from the fences and other buildings. In hot climatic conditions it is good to choose places which have shade from apart from the intense afternoon sunlight. It is always possible to keep a healthy garden with ten to 12 hours of sunlight; however, the plants must be quite adaptable. While the soil could always be improved, site with better soil is nevertheless a plus. Areas having rocky soil, or steep slopes, or the areas where water is stagnant must be avoided.

Then is the fun part of starting to dig. Gardening is never a clean hobby; one would definitely have to get dirt under the nails. Firstly the rocks, debris, along with grass and weeds must be removed. Then the spot up must be dug about a foot deep. We must then level up dirt and put in compost or minerals if needed. If the soil is very acidic, lime could be added. Now if it gets too sandy the some peat moss may be added. Plants would thrive in neutral with acidic soil when a little fertilizer is added.

If seeds are bought then they must be planted according to directions suggested. If you are picking plants then always choose those with green, and healthy looking stems leaves and healthy roots. Keep the smaller plants to the front of the bed. Keep the larger ones at the back. The key to successful start in gardening is ensuring the planting activity at the apt time.

Ascertain and wait till frosts are finished before planting. While planting the seeds always check the package. It would usually tell the exact time when you could plant them so as to achieve full growth.

As you have start and get into gardening, make sure that your plants get enough water essential for their growth.

Watering, especially hand watering would work well if there are only a few plants. Many other options would include things like sprinklers or the sprinkler hoses. During the cooler part of the day, watering is very effective. Amount of water required would depend on the type of plant; however most require an inch per week. When it is hottest period, the plants would need watering about three times in a week.

Mulch or compost is the most helpful of many things which could be added to a garden. A few inches of the organic mulch would improve fertility helping the soil to hold moisture. The wood chips, leaves, grass clippings, manure, and the pine needles are everything that could be used like the mulch.

RAISED SUMMER GARDENS

Raised gardens have become very popular as quite many of them are renting their property or finding themselves in the high rise apartments of buildings with some or no lawn space at all and moreover very less access to real soil to plant flowers and vegetables which they desire having with them. Actually, there are very few pros about using the raised gardens when opposed to tilling soil for those wishing to structure smaller gardens and also are limited about the space where it could be done. Simultaneously, those who wish for bigger yields are usually dissatisfied with limits of the raised gardens. Such are ultimately individual choices but it is suggested to know and point out a few of the pros and cons about such types of gardens so that people could decide about the same.

Soil compaction

The plants could love to breath. This is often very difficult when it is placed in the garden rows as there is a little bit of difficulty perhaps, avoiding all together possibility of stepping in the tilled rows where the fruits, vegetables, or the plants are planted in traditional garden situation. With the help of raised gardens, which are designed to be worked without, there is almost no fear of compacting soil around plants. During the same time most lifelong gardeners get a feel of the inability to walk in the gardens. This is a disadvantage as they prefer being able to do it. It is often matters about the preference than practicality but a valid opposition is just the same.

Numbers

You could essentially plant many plants in same amount of the square footage in the raised bed as there is no requirement for rows. One should also be very aware about the fact that the plants in the raised beds very often tend growing larger than those plants in the traditional garden rows. This being said one must resist the urge of over planting within raised garden beds. This would eliminate the slight benefit. Most traditional gardeners often see the results of having the beds overcrowded and feel that their manner of doing it is much better.

A good benefit to raise beds for the summer gardens in the areas which are almost saturated with the excess moisture is that, the raised beds would allow a better drainage than any traditional row gardening. It is one thing which the average gardener would not prefer arguing with, unless he lives in area where this is not much problem. Many gardeners in south though, where good deal of humidity is present along with some moisture, would agree that a proper drainage would be a problem.

The raised beds are quite less back breaking. It is a great benefit to a few of us who feel the years being crept into our bones. When we are above ground, the raised gardens offer much easier access for the activities of planting, weeding, and investigating for the signs of pests. A great thing about the raised garden is that they manifest to be slow and are not very quick to cool like the earth. It renders them much more productive and longer growing seasons like most of the gardens which are placed in ground.

Those of who have unusually shaped the yards or the growing areas, the raised gardens would allow the opportunity of having one beautiful summer garden almost in any shape you could build this box for. It means that you are never limited to rows, as many gardens often tend to be. You also have few more choices for aesthetics as you plan and grow the summer garden.

A downside to a raised summer garden is that it is very difficult to have it dismantled and almost impossible to till. It means one must do every working of soil by plain hands and most gardeners would not completely appreciate the look of the process. One most vital thing however, is about choosing the summer garden system which works best for you. Some may find combining the 2 would provide still better results. It is a good use of the time or you may also prefer one when compared to the other. As a matter of fact, there is no wrong answer in general. The wrong one would only be wrong for you.

LANDSCAPING YOUR SUMMER GARDEN

Quite many things should be considered as you plan and plant the summer garden. An important thing is natural landscape or the terrain of the lawn and the garden area. Whenever possible, it would be great to work with landscape than working totally against it or going towards extraordinary efforts in making changes to natural landscape of the lawn as one can quite easily and very beautifully plan the summer garden and go with flow working well along with natural terrain of the lawn and also garden area.

A way in which it can be accomplished is by taking quick surveys of the lawn. This would be more than any cursory visual survey. One would need to walk the lawn and the corresponding area in which the garden space is being planned to be implemented. You would need to measure terrains and take notes of the inclines and slopes. When one is at it, they must study the conditions of soil and check if there are areas which seem particularly inhospitable to plant. When such types of areas exist in the garden one must decide what should be done about them. We should check if it possible turning the patch into water feature or similar other attractive addition in the garden than having some bare patch in midst of flowers, plants, and vegetables.

One must also determine the right amount of shade a particular place would receive and, how shade can be created for those plants, flowers and vegetables when in the direct sunlight.

Indirect sunlight suits well to few plants. This could be accomplished if we plant them creatively within shadows of plants, shrubs, and vegetables which grow quite taller or even by using the rocks for creating shade. Climbing vines on the trellises or the fences so as to create artificial shade is also suggested.

After we have good feel for terrain and the landscape of our summer garden we would need planning for vegetables, flowers, and plants which would be used. The vegetable gardens tend to be not very aesthetic in nature often being the easiest for landscaping, as it is more of a need than some beauty. If one is planting some flowery summer garden, it is likely that they are planning to bring in some degree of exotic beauty in their garden. In this case it could be decided if one wants to keep flowers and plants in a specific color scheme or also if dramatic blues or greens require combining with some bright and vivid yellows and reds. This would be a personal decision but would affect greatly upon the appearance of one's garden when things are said and done.

One may landscape the garden according to amount of actual time and the effort available for devoting towards working on your garden in a given week. Few plants need more care than few others. If you are looking for a garden basically the sow and go type, then you must make sure it gets filled with flowers and plants suited for that kind of low maintenance. Many vegetable gardens need good deals of tending so as to flourish and cannot be acceptable in such situations.

If you are totally lost about landscaping the summer garden, you may find it beneficial and worth the effort having a team of experts coming in and doing the landscaping for your garden. When procuring the services ensure to check either into the maintenance program with them to keep up landscaping or get them to provide with a low maintenance kind of landscaping which you would be able to keep up with and duplicate upon your own.

Gardeners find tasks of landscaping the summer garden to be highlights of the growing summer season. Even if anyone is not among those, the above suggestions are always recommended to give you a good start along with other helpful tips about getting the garden landscaped; ready to grow.

OAK GARDEN FURNITURE

The most recognized among the manufacturers of Oak-Garden Furniture are Amish from Loudonville in Ohio. They make use of the North American Red Oak or the Cherry to structure the beautiful Garden Furniture which is great for the patio. The tops, face, sides, face-frame and the shelves are made of solid oak or the cherry wood, although pieces of the oak and cherry veneers might be used. Amish is proud to proclaim no particleboard or no pressboard, and not even masonite materials are used on any of their furniture and only real oak is grown in their own property.

Natural variations in the solid wood grain help to make cherry and the oak furniture very beautiful. Every piece of the Garden Oak Furniture would have unique characteristics as oak wood grains vary in its color. As you use natural wood stains the coloring would vary. If consistent color is required then one must use a varied stain.

Amish usually maintain a topcoat with exquisite catalyzed clear finish and a satin sheen. It appears like a hand-rubbed finishing of satin, though offers good protection including resistance from the spills as varied as vinegar, water, coffee, and even the paint thinner. It would allow you to use the furniture with a peace of mind; cleanup being real simple. You may use warm soap wash-cloth and this furniture cleans quite easily. Almost every piece of the Garden Furniture designed by the Amish Craftsmen is built in small shops with the use of old attention for the detail. This is the reason for people to go for Amish furniture about the Oak Garden Furniture durability and quality durability guaranteed. Beautiful settings for the patio come from keeping the Oak Garden Furniture.

Cedar Stations offer Chinese Oak furniture at affordable prices and the shipping is free too. Oak Adirondack Chair often comes partially assembled along with solid brass hardware. Solid Chinese Oak usually is stained with light oil for the lasting weather protection. The Cedar Station offers varieties in Java Indonesian Teak, Western Red Cedar, and also the Chinese Oak outdoor furniture. The Chinese oak is dense but finely-grained hardwood which is 5% harder compared to red oak. Cedar Station is very proud to offer the Oak Outdoor Furniture with all pieces of Chinese Oak, using the industry standard tenon joinery and mortise. This would prevent weakening of hinges, when left outdoors. The Chinese Oak dried to prevent cupping and warping. Lot of craftsmanship gets used for creating the beautiful Garden Patio Furniture set. It however, maybe bought for around a $100 with shipping free.

At Cedar Station many of the exquisite outdoor furniture gets made from teak, oak, and cedar. All types of the patio seating, the dining chairs, the Adirondack chairs, various benches, the rocking chairs, exotic porch swings, and others are made. The use this Chinese Oak makes products cheaper with the similar look as the oak from actual trees. Such oak gets farmed so that the forests would not be used and would protect the ecology of the earth. Whether one uses the Amish Oak or Chinese Oak outdoor furniture, it would last for a very long and good time making the patio to be envied.

PICKING A HEALTHY PLANT

As it comes to starting the garden, people have 2 choices; planting the seeds, or buying complete plants. Each idea has its own benefits. If seeds are planted and you and care for them daily, you would find it as a more rewarding experience when there is a full and healthy plant.

This method however, is quite risky. We often go about planting many seeds and never see its trace in future, whatsoever.

If the choice is about buying the plant from nursery and then installing it in the garden, it would reduce lots of work involved in keeping it healthy. In the past it has been found that many incompetent workers in the nursery workers would ruin the plant's future by putting varied chemicals and fertilizers on it. People have adapted to such incompetence by knowing to choose among the healthiest plants in the bunch. Below discussed are few of the techniques used in the screening process for the plants.

It would sound too superficial, but one thing people need to check about the prospective plants is if they really look nice. As far as the plants go, one could truly judge books by its cover. When the plant has been treated good and healthy having no diseases or pests, we could almost always tell looking at its good looks. When a plant grows up in unhealthy soil, or has some harmful bugs present in it, you could tell from its holey leaves and the wilted stems.

When browsing the shelves in the nursery looking for the dream plant, you would want to exclude things that presently have flowers. The plants are very less traumatized by transplants if they don't presently have flowers. It is great to check ones that just has the buds. But when you are supposed to choose from all flowering plants, then you must do the unthinkable and sever each one of them. It would be worth it when plant's future health is concerned. Transplanting the plant when it blooms would result in dead plants; around 90 percent of the times.

Make sure to check the roots as you plop the money down to purchase the plant. If incase the roots are in real terrible condition you would be able to realize looking at the remaining plant. But when the roots are only slightly out of structure, then you probably would not be able to say just by having a look at it. You must inspect the roots too close for every signs of rottenness, brownness, or softness. Roots must always be firm, and should act as a perfectly well staged infrastructure holding all soils together. One could easily say if roots are before or past the prime, depending upon root and soil ratio. If there is a ridiculous amount of root with less soil, or bunch of soil with fewer roots, one should make sure to not buy the plant.

If there are any abnormalities found with the plant, be it the shape of roots or any other irregular features with leaves etc, you must ensure to ask the employees in the nursery. While often these things could be signs of unhealthy plants, at times there would be logical explanations about it. Give the nursery chances before you plan to write them off as horrendous. They are after all, professionals who deal with or have been dealing with several plants for years.

So if people decide to go about the easy route of getting plants from a nursery, they would just have to keep in mind about the health of plants as it is left up to others they don't know. Often they do good jobs, but people should always double check for their safety. Also every precaution must be taken to avoid transplant shocks in plants when they have trouble adjusting to the new location; leading to health problems in future. Very often the process goes well, but may never be too accurate about it.

PICKING THE IDEAL LOCATION
FOR YOUR GARDEN

As you decide about the garden you wish for, there are several other factors you would need to decide as you essentially get working with the gardening tools. Most importantly you would need to decide on its location. The location criterion is often decided by many factors. It depends on how one would water it or how much shade is needed, etc. Few of the questions could be very vital in deciding if your garden would live or die. Hence they should not be taken lightly. You must take each one in special consideration.

Deciding about the location of the garden in one's yard is an important thing to decide. One must choose a location which would provide ideal climatic conditions for all plants in the garden. Everything would depend up on the type of garden a person is dealing with and hence there is no standard or specific advice. Hence, when you Google search about the plant you are dealing with you would find plethora of sites telling you about the right conditions for its growth. After this, it is only a matter of checking the most shaded and the sunniest spot within your yard.

A deciding factor asks about how one may plan with regards watering one's garden. If one has a sprinkler system readily installed for the grass, then it might be a better idea to put the garden in midst of the yard. Then it would even get watered all at one time, and would need no extra toil from your part. However, if this does not provide the right location for the garden, then one might end up watering it by hose or by dragging a sprinkler there. In such cases, just ensure that your garden is in an ideal distance for any hose to reach. This might not show up as a good thing for basing the overall location of the garden on; however, you would be surprised and happy about having it planned out in advance.

Bringing in some right amount of shade in your garden could be a difficult task. As you get a basic idea about where you need your garden, you may perhaps want to keep watching it and record the number of hours it would spend in sunlight and the number of hours it would spend in shade. You may compare the findings to some online web site. You must then be able to determine if the spot chosen is ideal for planting and consequently starting your garden. The amount would indeed change just like how the seasons change. This should give a good idea about what one can basically expect for the remaining year. If required, later you could put up some sort of shade for protecting the garden from getting heavy sunlight.

After having determined some ideal place for the garden and if it has apt amount of sunlight, and if you would be able to conveniently have it watered, you are a step closer to factually starting a garden of your own. Of course, several other factors exists which are often overlooked here. Most of all, however, you must be able to check if the location chosen is good based on your common sense. One may simply think, "If I was to plant, would anything flourish here?" Honestly if your answer is yes, then you may think it is the time for heading out to the local gardening store and buying the required soil and fertilizer for getting started! It would apparently be a fun activity!

SUMMER GARDEN WEDDINGS

Blushing June brides usually want some things even more than some exotic fairy tale summer wedding in the garden surrounded by family, friends, and all the beautiful flowers. One may find many ways to create and plan beautiful summer garden wedding which most brides usually dream about if they are willing to take risks of the weather whim in order to make the dream come true. It is true that the gods may dare to call forth rain on weddings of beautiful June brides

One would not only need to account the scope and size of summer gardens which are question during the plan of a wedding but even the access to interior spots suitable for wedding; in case things go wrong or Mother Nature allowing few stray drops of rain on the parade. The factor of rain makes the brides to plan for the arrangements of tents for the fateful day. It would protect all those who would attend and also the ceremony.

One must consider clothing too, for the summer garden wedding. The idea of some formal attire for this wedding may look beautiful and also appealing but you should ensure to carefully consider reality of potentially higher temperatures which may be compounded with humidity and such effects staying upon the air, make up, the trappings which go along with some formal attire and also tuxedos. This may be little too hot for the comfort concerned as you are confronted with bright sunny summer afternoon. Look for the clothing with care and prepare for fans on hand if the members of bride or groom's party are overheated.

A reason for most brides to elect having a garden wedding in summer is because they may be less formal than being a little more. This would mean that concessions could be made in most places when it about formality and summer atmosphere and entire wedding could be more relaxed and a fun occasion than some sober ceremony which many try making it to be.

Consequently, another good thing about the summer garden wedding is using flowers from the same garden where you are planning to get married. This way the bouquet may be created. It would no doubt provide lots of bright and beautiful choices allowing the party getting blended with appropriate natural surroundings. This would also help the budget-conscious brides saving the extra money as it comes towards the cost of weddings.

An important thing that is considered while planning summer weddings in the garden is the comfort of your guests. You must plan for places where guests could cool off making sure there are quite many drinks flowing which would keep them from the very possibility of dehydrating. Ample number of bottled water upon ice is a great plan for weddings in summer or a summer garden wedding. Ensure plenty of water for keeping the bridal party, the groom and the groomsmen well hydrated before and after the real occurrence of ceremony.

A final bit of counseling for the summer garden wedding is taking time and literally sitting back smelling the roses and many other flowers which may be present. A part of beauty in the garden wedding is all about the myriad of fragrances which are filling in the air. One must take time to enjoy smaller things like this which make the day very special for happy couples and all others who share such special events.

UNDERSTANDING CONTAINER GARDENING

If you happen to be a garden lover and have hardly any space for the gardening appetite, you need not worry as gardening is definitely within your reach. Within the available area of the house; be it a balcony, a patio, deck, or some sunny window, you could create the container gardening, which would not just bring in joy but the vegetables too. You may very well be ready to start the container gardening all by yourself.

During the past, gardening was an exclusive realm of landowners. These days even the flat dwellers may grow their dream garden without having much fuss. A dream could be fulfilled by the container gardening, which would mean gardening in some special container. The art of container gardening would give great delights of the landscape without any weekly mowing. In containers, you could raise few perennials, annuals, or even shrubs and some small trees.

Do not think that the container gardening could be achieved quite easily. Container gardening too requires good planning similar to that of the traditional gardening type. The planning would consist of finding the USDA zone which would help to identify suitable plant variety in your zone, right amount of daylight one is receiving in the apartment, and then choose the beloved plant variety.

Buying the plants is always advisable from the nearest nursery until you have the right conditions for going about the indoor seedlings. One should not keep tender plants of the container gardening outside, i.e., below 45° F temperature or in the soaring winds. Furthermore, one must not leave the new plants all through the night outside, as it might get frost out.

There are false notions that every plant which grows in the ground would not grow in container gardening. It is never so. When you have such doubts, it is highly recommended to experiment on the same. Furthermore, any container with few holes for the drainage could be used for the container gardening.

The field of container gardening would need little budget during the initial stages. But this would be like having low maintenance and good satisfaction. This kind of gardening would require less fertilizer and water as per the specific plant requirements.

There are several pot growing varieties of vegetable similar to the container gardening. In such kinds, the vegetable plant would need only good sunlight and water. When these things are provided, it would easily help in getting good vegetables for the ratatouille and salads. You could get better satisfaction as you serve these varieties nurtured with your own hands to all your beloved pals.

Do not ever despair if you are not having a balcony or deck? You could get a nod from the landlord for the window boxes for modern container gardening. One may make it highly possible about growing several bloomy annuals all year-round with indoor vegetables in the sunny window. Besides, there is yet another type of a garden called as the community gardens, which would satisfy all city dwellers.

There would be no need for ending the container gardening as you enter autumn. You could continue with your container gardening as you must select the plants which withholds the frost. Common plant varieties which stands up to the frost are Mexican feather grass, Eulalie grasses, Cornflowers, Lavender cottons, Stonecrops, Jasmine, Million bells, etc.,

For extending the life of the garden from an early spring to fall, one could replant matching the conditions. One may even contact some of America's finest gardeners through the internet for better designs in case of your container gardening. These gardeners offer suggestions like caring and choosing the pots, the growing tips for the roses, succulents, and the bulbs, in containers.

Printed by Libri Plureos GmbH in Hamburg,
Germany